My State
NEW MEXICO

By Christina Earley

TABLE OF CONTENTS

A Crabtree Seedlings Book

School-to-Home Support for Caregivers and Teachers

This book helps children grow by letting them practice reading. Here are a few guiding questions to help the reader build his or her comprehension skills. Possible answers appear in red.

Before Reading:

- What do I know about New Mexico?
    - *I know that New Mexico is a state.*
    - *I know that New Mexico has mountains.*
- What do I want to learn about New Mexico?
    - *I want to learn which famous people were born in New Mexico.*
    - *I want to learn what the state flag looks like.*

During Reading:

- What have I learned so far?
    - *I have learned that Santa Fe is the state capital of New Mexico.*
    - *I have learned that there is no running water or electricity in Taos Pueblo.*
- I wonder why...
    - *I wonder why the state flower is the yucca flower.*
    - *I wonder why the Ah-Shi-Sle-Pah Wilderness looks like a different planet.*

After Reading:

- What did I learn about New Mexico?
    - *I have learned that you can sled down the sand dunes at White Sands National Park.*
    - *I have learned that the state animal is the black bear.*
- Read the book again and look for the glossary words.
    - *I see the word **capital** on page 6, and the word **adobe** on page 14. The other glossary words are found on pages 22 and 23.*

NEW MEXICO
Hi! My name is Alex. Welcome to New Mexico!
GALLERY
Quesadilla GRILLE
WELCO

I live in Deming. I can see the Florida Mountains from my house.

The Great American Duck Race is held every year in my city.

New Mexico is in the southwestern United States. The **capital** is Santa Fe.

Fun Fact: Albuquerque is the largest city in New Mexico.

The state animal is the black bear.

The yucca flower is the state flower.

We grow a lot of chile peppers in New Mexico. Some of them are used to make hot sauce.
HOT Sauce

Fun Fact: New Mexico grows around 51,000 tons (46,000 metric tons) of chile peppers a year.

My state flag is yellow. The **Zia sun** symbol is in the middle.

Watching the Albuquerque Isotopes play baseball is exciting!

Taos Pueblo is an **ancient** village made from **adobe**. **Pueblo peoples** still live in this village.

Fun Fact: There is no running water or electricity inside the village.

Sledding down the sand dunes at White Sands National Park is exciting.

I like to explore the caves at Carlsbad Caverns National Park.

Jeff Bezos, the founder of Amazon, was born in New Mexico. Singer Demi Lovato was also born in New Mexico.

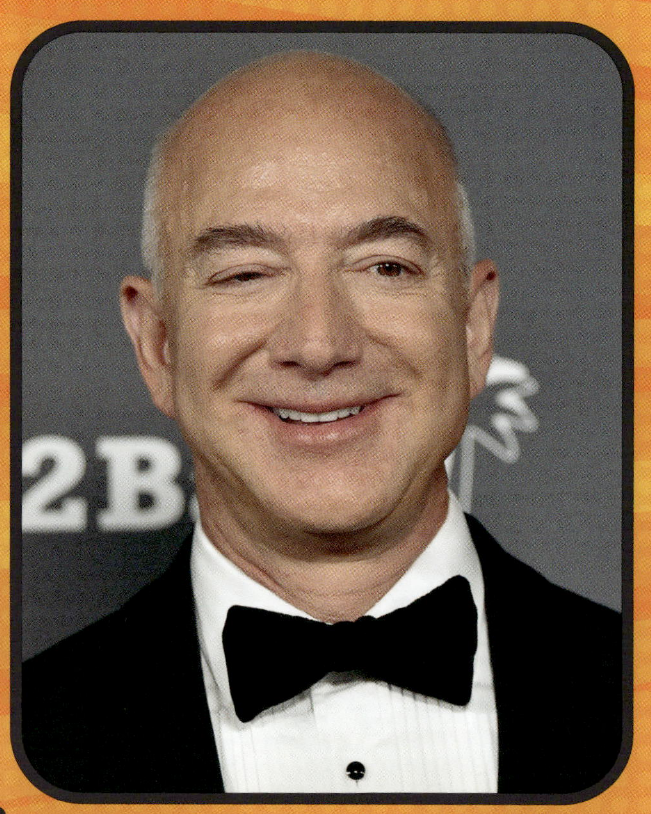

Fun Fact: **Activist** Dolores Huerta was born in Dawson, New Mexico.

I like to go skiing with my family at Taos Ski Valley.

I pretend I am on another planet in the Ah-Shi-Sle-Pah Wilderness.

Glossary

activist (ak-tuh-vist): A person who works to bring about changes in politics or society

adobe (uhd-oh-bee): A type of building material made from mud and straw

ancient (ayn-chent): Very old

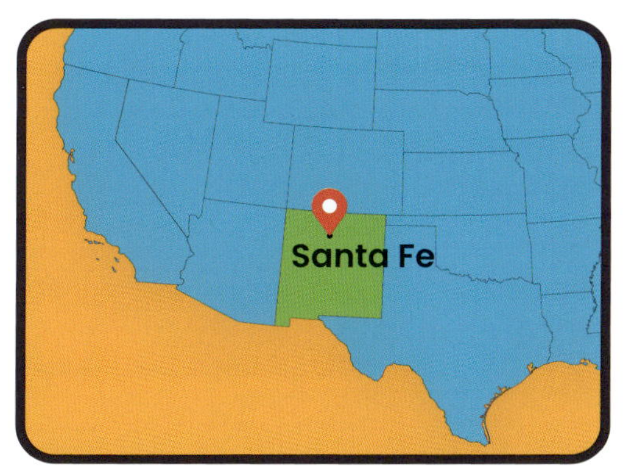

capital (cap-ih-tuhl): The city or town where the government of a country, state, or province is located

Pueblo peoples (pweb-loh pee-puhls): A group of Native American peoples living in the southwest United States

Zia sun (zee-uh suhn): A symbol that originated with the Zia Native American peoples, consisting of a red circle with four sets of four rays pointing in four directions

Index

About the Author

Christina Earley lives in sunny South Florida with her husband and son. She enjoys traveling around the United States and learning about different historical places. Her hobbies include hiking, yoga, and baking.

Written by: Christina Earley
Designed and Illustrated by: Bobbie Houser
Series Development: James Earley
Proofreader: Melissa Boyce
Educational Consultant: Marie Lemke M.Ed.

Photographs:
Alamy: Efrain Padro: p. 13
Shutterstock: sunsinger: cover; Sean Pavone: p. 3, 7, 21; Witold Skrypczak: p. 4; Daniel Dupuis: p. 5; Volina: p. 6, 23; Dennis W Donohue: p. 8; Cristina Ohler: p. 9; khan3145: p. 10-11; Raisa Nastukova: p. 11; railway fx: p. 12, 23; Gimas: p. 14-15, 22-23; Vineyard Perspective: p. 15; IrinaK: p. 16; Doug Meek: p. 17; DFree: p. 18 left; Ben Houdijk: p. 18 right; Eugene Powers: p. 19, 22; Roschetzky Photography: p. 20

Crabtree Publishing

crabtreebooks.com 800-387-7650

Printed in the U.S.A./072023/CG20230214

Published in Canada
Crabtree Publishing
616 Welland Avenue
St. Catharines, Ontario
L2M 5V6

Published in the United States
Crabtree Publishing
347 Fifth Avenue
Suite 1402-145
New York, New York, 10016

Library and Archives Canada Cataloguing in Publication
Available at Library and Archives Canada

Library of Congress Cataloging-in-Publication Data
Available at the Library of Congress

Hardcover: 978-1-0398-0528-6
Paperback: 978-1-0398-0560-6
Ebook (pdf): 978-1-0398-0624-5
Epub: 978-1-0398-0592-7